THAT WE MAY BE ONE

THAT WE MAY BE
one

CHRISTIAN NON-DUALITY

Thomas Keating

FOREWORD BY CYNTHIA BOURGEAULT

WAYFARER BOOKS
SAN JUAN MOUNTAINS, COLORADO

WAYFARER BOOKS
SAN JUAN MOUNTAINS, COLORADO

First Edition Published in 2024 by Wayfarer Books
Cover Design and Interior Design by Connor Wolfe
TRADE PAPERBACK 978-1-956368-98-7

10 9 8 7 6 5 4 3 2 1

WHOLESALE INQUIRIES? You can find our books available via Ingram, offered with standard trade terms and lifetime returnability. With printing bases in the US, the EU, the UK, and Australia, Wayfarer has the capability to fulfill orders globally. Our titles are available wherever books are sold in paperback, ebook, and audiobook. Find our books at local Indies, Bookshop.org, iTunes, Barnes & Noble, Amazon > US & International, or direct at wayfarerbookstore.com.

WAYFARERBOOKS.ORG
WAYFARERMAGAZINE.COM
WAYFARERBOOKSTORE.COM

SUPPORTING INDIGENOUS FUTURES
1% GIVEN BACK

Open Mind, Open Heart

God is All in All

God is Love

The Gift of Lfe

Heartfulness

Manifesting God

Intimacy with God

Invitation to Love

The Human Condition

The Mystery of Christ

Awakenings

Reawakenings

Crisis of Faith, Crisis of Love

The Better Part

The Transformation of Suffering

The Heart of the World

Finding Grace at the Center

CONTENTS

xiii   Foreword by Cynthia Bourgeault

1   Chapter One
The Western and Scriptural Models of Spirituality

7   Chapter Two
The Invitation of the Christian Contemplative Tradition

15   Chapter Three
The Self and Evolving Consciousness

25   Chapter Four
Christian Non-duality and Unity Consciousness

33   Chapter Five
The Present Moment and All That Is

41   Chapter Six
Fallen, Beloved, Surrendered

51   Further Reflections

55   Guidelines for Christian Life,
Growth & Transformation
from *Open Mind, Open Heart*

I speak this in the world so that they may share my joy completely...As you sent me into the world, so I send them into the world. And I consecrate myself for them, so that they may be consecrated in truth... So that they may all be one, as you, Father, are in me and I in you, that they may be in us...I have given them the glory you gave me, so that they may be one, as we are one, I in them and you in me, that they many be brought to perfection as one, that the world may know you sent me, and that you love them even as you loved me. Father, they are your gift to me. I wish that where I am they also may be with me...that the love with which you have loved me may be in them and I in them."

—JESUS OF NAZARETH, *Gospel of John*

*Trust in me with your life because I am you,
more than you are yourself.*

– Bhagavad Gita

FOREWORD

by Cynthia Bourgeault

Thomas Keating once reportedly quipped to one of his Vedanta colleagues, "Contemplative Outreach is my day job; the interspiritual dialogue is my night job." He knew full well—and accepted fully—that his major vocational task in this life was to assist in the contemplative renewal of Christianity, awakening his fellow Christians to the contemplative treasures hidden in their own backyard. He executed this task wisely and well, both by helping to create the method of Centering Prayer and through his imaginative reframing of traditional spiritual teaching in "an updated format" (as he called it), accessible to lay people working in the world. He held the post faithfully for more than forty years, inviting a whole new generation of Christians to awaken to what he called "the contemplative dimension of the Gospel."

Almost from the beginning of his religious career, however, he had also experienced a strong attraction to the
unitive teaching of other faith traditions—not so much
in order to make up for something he felt missing in his
own, but to find his deepest unitive openings affirmed
and mirrored in the less dualistic and less propositional
languages of most of the non-Christian spiritual traditions. Even in his early days as abbot of St. Joseph's
Abbey (1961-81) he had come to see the contemplative
path as a common treasury of all the great religions, and
he was already drawing upon resources from these other traditions to deepen contemplative practice within
his own Trappist community. In 1984, the same year
that he founded Contemplative Outreach, he also host-
ed the first Snowmass Conference: a small invitational
gathering of contemplatives from a number of different spiritual traditions (Buddhist, Orthodox, Islamic,
Jewish, Hindu), the only agenda being to meditate together and share conversation from the heart. These
two outreaches—Contemplative Outreach and the
Snowmass Conference—nurtured him, fed him, sus-
tained and cross-pollinated his own spiritual life. He
came alive in each circle in different ways.

For most of his long career, he kept his "day job" and "night job" carefully differentiated, addressing his Christian audience in the more traditional theological categories and contemporary psychological language that would open doors rather than close them. In his "night job," he continued to forage voraciously within the unitive traditions of the world. Particularly after his retirement from active teaching duty, he returned to his old wellsprings: the Christian nondual mystics and contemporary Hindu or Hindu-Christian masters such as Ramana Maharshi and Bede Griffiths. He remained deeply engaged with the work on the evolution of consciousness emerging from his longtime friend Ken Wilber and combined this with a growing interest in the findings of contemporary neuroscience and the groundbreaking work of the Mind and Life Institute, established by His Holiness the Dalai Lama, also a personal friend. "By night" he was actively seeking new frameworks of understanding and new pathways of unity.

At some point during the last five years of his life, the two streams of his life began to flow together. He dived into the river and simply let it carry him. Beginning about 2014 with his remarkable book *Reflections on the*

Unknowable, he is clearly and with increasing radiance speaking from a different place: as a realized Christian master, his mind and heart grounded in unity consciousness, his feet firmly planted in Christian soil.

In the summer of 2016 Thomas invited a few friends in his interspiritual circle to St. Benedict's Monastery for an intimate and wide-ranging conversation on Non-duality from a Christian perspective. This present volume, *That We May Be One,* is the fruit of that conversation, skillfully refashioned by his longtime editor Mary Anne Best into six short, reflective essays. The result is no doubt Thomas's most comprehensive teaching on Non-duality from the perspective of evolutionary consciousness. In this slender volume he seems to to pull out all the stops, sidestepping most traditional Christian starting points in order to speak directly from what he has come to know from an evolutionary perspective about Non-duality, levels of consciousness, the shortcomings of traditional Western spiritual models, present moment awareness, and the journey from rational consciousness and ego-selfhood into something he calls "unity consciousness," experienced both as an interior state and as an exterior manner of living in this world. It is, to say the least, a remarkable synthesis.

He begins by introducing Non-duality (a term not native to the traditional Christian spiritual lexicon) as a functional synonym for what other spiritual traditions describe as "awakening" or "enlightenment." For those wishing an immediate Christian counterpart he suggests "the transforming union," but makes it clear that he is not going be approaching this in the traditional way—as a more intimate affective union—but rather, as a whole new level of consciousness. His argument in a nutshell is that Non-duality cannot be attained at our familiar, rational level of consciousness and by the ego-selfhood joined at the hip to it. It requires the shift to a higher level of consciousness—unity consciousness—which for Thomas is the direct perception of the oneness of everything. Non-duality represents an evolutionary leap—not just for our personal self-realization, but for our collective humanity.

As the streams of his thinking continue to flow together, he seamlessly positions contemplative prayer as a powerful driveshaft of this evolution. "If we are experiencing God as more intimate and more available, we move to higher levels of consciousness," he writes. Since he has taught from the very beginning that this is exactly what contemplative prayer is intended to do—i.e., to lead us into a more intimate, wordless communion with God—he is effectively repositioning this kind of prayer as a powerful vehicle for the evolution of human consciousness. In this book Centering Prayer definitively "graduates" from being simply a catalytic tool for personal healing and transformation and re-emerges as the royal road to planetary oneness, all the more indispensable because it is so immediately accessible.

As is typical in these final works of Thomas Keating, the most jaw-dropping insights are often buried in simple one-liners, aphorisms, or even "throw-aways." In this book, you'll hear him speaking for the first time of something he calls "the ultimate self." "The ultimate self is beyond the True Self," he writes, "It is the Word of God manifesting in our particular human weakness." Also in this book, reflecting insights first articulated by Bernadette Roberts in her ground-breaking No-Self books, he notices that "Being aware of ourselves and of God is a kind of duality. Even in the transforming union we are still two." He also affirms that "the ultimate consciousness is the total Oneness in which God is all in all." Flinging his cosmic mysticism to the outermost limits, he writes:

So much for the self that becomes God's Self, or One with God's Self, or just plain One. All the mystics agree that it is totally inconceivable. All words can only point in the direction of the Ultimate Reality and the highest experience in this life cannot do justice to "Isness" itself.

But have no fears that Thomas has gone missing in the infinite! If he opens up these occasional peepholes into the ineffable vastness that was calling to his heart in those final years of his life, it is only to draw us back more firmly to the particulars of the place we occupy here and now, in a fragile and imperiled planet. Oneness for him is not a future utopia but a present imperative, the alternative being, as he often starkly put it, "human-icide." To the extent that contemplation is a vehicle for the evolution of consciousness (as he so forcefully argues here), it falls particularly on those of us seeking to walk this path to share the fruits of this work with a planet literally dying for lack of it. And it is just here, of course, that Thomas' "day job" and "night job" finally converge completely in a single stream of unified compassionate action. The fruits of this synthesis are here before you in this book, and I trust that you will receive them with both the full seriousness and signature gentle touch with which they were offered.

Oneness was the final mantra of Thomas Keating's life. It pervades all his late teaching and writing even as it flows from his being itself. This book is not casually titled. It contains his final and deepest prayer: that both inwardly and outwardly we might indeed become one, allowing the inner radiance of our own transformed being to suffuse the dry bones of this world in order that it might yet reveal itself as "the Mystical Body of Christ," the ultimate shape of unity as it can be lived in manifest form.

–Cynthia Bourgeault

AUTUMN 2023

Forsake everything that is yours. Undertake this, and let it cost you everything you can afford. There you will find true peace, and nowhere else.

Never think too much about what you could do, but about what you could be.

As we are holy and have being, to that extent we make all works holy, be it eating, sleeping, keeping vigil or whatever it may be.

What matters is the ground on which the works are built.

— MEISTER ECKHART

CHAPTER ONE

The Western and Scriptural Models of Spirituality

God, Self and Rational Consciousness

Non-duality is becoming a household word in places where inter-spiritual dialogue is a familiar phenomenon. This is a significant issue for all religions; I will focus on how it affects our Christian understanding and the transformative process. Non-duality is a synonym for awakening or enlightenment, as expressed in other spiritual traditions.

We need to keep in mind that the Christian tradition, especially since the Reformation, has focused on doctrinal differences between the denominations rather than on the spiritual journey itself and actually practicing the contemplative dimension of the Gospel.

In recent years Richard Hauser, a Jesuit professor at Creighton University, described the Western Model of Spirituality as compared with the Scriptural Model of Spirituality. The Western Model is based on seeing Christian spirituality as the self-outside-of-God.

The Christian mystics, from Pseudo-Dionysius, *The Cloud of Unknowing,* Ruysbroeck, Eckhart and the Dominicans, the Beguines of the 13th century, taught the self is in God.

Thus, there is a basic conflict in Christianity itself. In the last several hundred years priests have rarely been taught about the contemplative dimension of the Gospel or the Christian mystical tradition. The most they could usually find in a university or a seminary was the history of Christian spirituality.

In scriptural spirituality we are to become a sacrament of the presence of God. This presence is not a Sunday affair. It's not a goodnight prayer, or a wakeup prayer. It's all the time. That is the goal of the Christian life as laid-out in the Gospels. We are in God and our actions are to be motivated by the Spirit's movement, inspiration, and guidance within us into oneness with the Trinity.

The Western Model of God-outside-of-self describes a relationship that is at odds with the Gospel teaching. Until the beginning of the Second Vatican Council we rarely heard the doctrine that we are in God and that God is in us. This led to the idea, especially in Protestant circles, that God really was displeased with us.

The Scriptural Model acknowledges our sins, but says very clearly that Christ has come to take them away and to unite us with himself. We cannot possibly exist without God being in us since God is everywhere. Although theology taught this doctrine in the Middle Ages, it was the mystics who took it seriously and grasped what it meant.

Here are some of the symptoms of the Western Model of Spirituality: We initiate our good efforts and God rewards. Thus, we have an image of God sitting in the bleachers of an arena watching our activities. If they are good, it's thumbs up! If they are not, it's thumbs down. Grace in the Western Model enables us to build-up rewards in Heaven, as long as we keep earning them through our good works.

In the Scriptural Model, grace is present not only in the sacraments in a special way, but inspires our good actions. In the Western Model, we do all the work even though influenced by reflections on Scripture. There is, however, a deep psychological distrust of ourselves. We are just too "bad" and unworthy of God's love for us. In daily life, a lot of what we do does not seem to have anything to do with God.

In the theological principles in *Open Mind, Open Heart* our basic core of goodness is emphasized. Some who have been trained in the Calvinistic tradition are shocked by that statement because, in their understanding, followers of Christ put on holiness like a cloak, but their evil human nature persists underneath the cloak. Those eager for transformation in Christ as presented in the Spiritual Model and those who seek the reward of Heaven for their good deeds in the Western Model are living in two different worlds.

Those who follow the Western Model have no idea what the mystics are talking about, or why people practice methods of meditation to cultivate interior silence and to experience the presence of the Ultimate Reality everywhere and in everything, including ourselves. As non-dual consciousness begins to unfold, so does the capacity for serving others and for seeing suffering not just as a problem but as a challenge.

If our consciousness is growing, conflicts are resolved, not on the rational level, the level of opposites and duality, but on the non-dual level. Apparent disasters and contradictions are perceived as invitations to move to a higher level of consciousness. There the two are resolved in the light of a higher perspective where they are not contradictory, but complimentary.

Leave your front door and your back door open.
Let thoughts come and go, just don't serve them tea.

—SHUNRYU SUZUKI

CHAPTER TWO

The Invitation of the Christian Contemplative Tradition

Beyond Rational Consciousness

What is Non-duality? Without contemplative centers, the Christian perspective was virtually lost in the church. Monasteries grew because there was no other place where you could go to find this dimension of the Gospel and intuitively devout people thought, "Oh, if only I could pick weeds or dig holes in the monastic garden, I would have a better chance of getting to Heaven." The intimacy, closeness, presence, and guidance of the Holy Spirit got to be more and more unknown.

When I was a boy, the Holy Spirit was known as the "forgotten guest" of the soul. How could we forget the infinite presence of Love? The solution is to develop and interiorize a personal relationship with Christ as the Incarnate Word and Son of God.

Many Christians are deprived of a deep faith in God's presence within them and the immense possibilities of the Christian life as presented by Jesus in his teaching and example. The intimacy that that implies is beyond any human intimacy that we can conceive of and is the source of our being at every moment. How important it is to integrate into this Infinite Reality that is beginning to be seen as not only the supreme Being, but Being beyond being. That is, "Isness" that has no limitation in any direction. Whatever you do, you are not only in the presence of God, but under the influence of the Spirit suggesting within us what the proper response to every detail of daily life actually is.

The extraordinary invitation of the Gospel to become one with God involves the gradual development of a consciousness beyond rational consciousness into what some spiritual traditions call "Non-duality." In the Christian mystical tradition this is usually called the transforming union. According to Saint John of the Cross, the Christian spiritual journey culminates in the transforming union. At that point there is no more domination of our sense or mental faculties over our conduct or thoughts. The Holy Spirit is the principle of our actions and love is the expression of the Spirit's action within us.

The transforming union is to become who you really are. Whatever happens to you then is seen as God's plan. You may be given an important apostolate. You may become ill and called to offer-up your suffering for God's people, or you just become old and offer this to God. Through these means we become in the deepest sense co-creators and co-redeemers with Christ.

Science, without intending it, has reinforced some of the great mystical intuitions of all time. American Franciscan nun and theologian Ilia Delio's explanation of spiritual evolution following the writings of French Jesuit priest and scientist Pierre Teilhard de Chardin is crucial to this idea of the stages of consciousness. God's diversity is manifested in the multitude of reactions of human beings. This diversity is not meant to lead to wars, as it has in human history, but to the enrichment of perceiving God from the infinite number of perspectives that human beings can perceive.

We cannot explain that level of consciousness without living it in some degree and fostering the Divine Indwelling. Centering Prayer is precisely our consent to God's presence and action within us, the Divine Indwelling and a way of preparing ourselves to receive.

On the level of rational consciousness, effort is all-important. Effort becomes a hindrance, however, to further development at a certain point when rationality turns into the realization of the self-in-God. Some of us are slow learners. The purpose of the Redemption of Christ was to go to the most extreme lengths to convince us that God is willing to do anything to make us participants in the divine nature, both now and in the world to come. What dies, in this perspective, is the body and the false self. The ultimate Self is beyond the True Self. It is the Word of God manifesting in our particular human uniqueness.

Even though God is within us, we do not deny the limitations of human nature with its weakness and proneness to selfishness. We make mistakes and we fail, but the relationship with God in the Christian perspective continues to develop. It gradually perceives that Ultimate Reality is love, and love is the most important activity that any creature can contribute to and that ultimately interests God.

As Saint John of the Cross puts it, "We will be judged on love."

The human race is a species that is completely interconnected and interrelated. It is one with God already. We just do not think so or experience it.

But some people have, like Merton in the street in Louisville, had this vision of the light that the Hindus speak of. He saw that light-up in all the people on the street and he could not help loving them all. Of course, it did not last, but God grants insights that will become permanent later on and which give us a huge boost forward in the transformative process.

Gregory of Nyssa says that in Heaven we go on growing in God forever. There is no lack of mansions, as Jesus put it, but there are different levels of penetrating the full possibilities of the human capacity for transformation. We learn from contemporary psychology about the stages of consciousness. We cannot be an adult without ceasing to be in adolescence.

Teilhard de Chardin thought that bodily evolution is pretty much over and now it is time to focus on spiritual evolution and higher stages of consciousness. If you seek enlightenment too ardently you are on the wrong path. It would be just another ego trip.

You cannot have any attachment to the process, so you try to possess nothing, have nothing, be nothing. Even after enlightenment, mystics strongly affirm there is a lot of spiritual work to be done.

As we grow spiritually, we move as human beings grow. A growth in one is usually a growth in the other. They are very interrelated. We have to die to the previous level, or if you prefer less strong language, you have to be moved into a bigger box, as if you were a holon. The holon theory means that you can move from being a particle all the way up to divine union. Each box is inside another box, so to speak. In order to grow, we have to let go of the limitations of the previous level we were on. This does not mean there was anything evil about it, but that we are being called to move to a new perspective. We keep all that was good in the lower level which is translated into the new capacity. For example, the molecule becomes a cell, and the cell an organ, and an organ, a part of the whole human body. Human consciousness can go on expanding right up to union with God. Science is becoming more and more a prophet for our time, telling us things about God we never knew and about how the universe works. It is reinforcing many mystical experiences of the past.

At the same time, we are in a body that is very fragile, and we have a will that has some measure of free choice, but is still very limited. The experience for most of life is a failure in varying degrees. In the Christian perspective, the exercise of faith is to keep trying, failing, and trying again. Although that practice is still part of the rational level of consciousness, it is a necessary foundation for the effortless activity of contemplative prayer that Saint John of the Cross describes as totally passive, at least when it is fully developed.

Like all other human experiences, God's relationship with every person is absolutely unique. In addition, we cannot negotiate the spiritual journey without a community to challenge us, to experience ourselves reacting with other people and seeing God in them, and exercising the kind of practical love that God manifests in helping us.

CHAPTER THREE

The Self and Evolving Consciousness

God is not just with us, not just beside us, not just under us, not just over us, but within us. What is the self? The only self we know is the false self that developed in infancy under the influence of the three emotional programs for happiness and especially under the influence of a separate-self sense. The infant, after six or eight months of depending on its mother, begins to realize that she is not going to do everything forever, so it begins to take care of itself. It then needs to feel secure, loved, and free to experience power and control in some degree.

The self is not an entity. Science has looked everywhere for a self in the human organism, but cannot find one. There is no central place of a physical nature that you can identify as the self. The child, when it moves to each new level of consciousness, has to let go of things that it liked in the previous stage. Now it no longer feels that they are necessary to maintain because of its new perspective. Every substantial change in consciousness provides a new perspective that requires time to integrate it into our present mind, body, emotions, and soul. God must know this.

God doesn't expect us to succeed at the first try, but waits for us and guides us. Through the Holy Spirit we have the greatest kind of psychotherapy that exists. The Spirit knows us through and through, knows the obstacles, and knows how much of our negative motivation is the result of the traumas of early childhood which make it hard to be charitable all the time. It is easy to react and want revenge.

Anybody who is on the spiritual journey is always wondering, "How do I get over my faults?" We may have to struggle with the temptation to give up the journey.

Then comes a big opening, and we move into a new level of consciousness. We work at that until we hit another plateau. Every major change seems to include the psychological experience of depression or discouragement before liberation and the experience of inner resurrection into a new level of consciousness. At each new level of growth, all our relationships change, especially our relationship to God.

The movement towards unity consciousness is experiencing the Divine as our ultimate Self, in which case the false self, ego, and sense of a separate self are laid to rest. Whatever happens then remains to be seen.

Nobody knows quite what the self is. Neuroscience is just as interested as spiritual seekers are. One theory is that the self, as we know it, is fluid and changes with each new level of consciousness, while maintaining its capacity for integrating this new information about itself and its relationships. The self then keeps growing and moves from the false self to the True Self.

There is the superficial self that we present to others that may include our resume, where we live, what we put down on paper for a doctor's visit.

Then there is the self as our personality and this is what makes us tick in ordinary relationships. It is the self you need to get to know, I presume, before you get married. The first one is "WHO are you?"

The second one is "Who ARE you?" The third one is, "Who are YOU?" And now you are on the spiritual journey.

If you accept the view that the self can keep on changing and growing, then it becomes the True Self in the image and likeness of God. Finally there is the experience that there is only one Self. If there is consciousness in God, it is shared with every creature according to its capacity. God is present in everyone, relating to them where they are, but nudging them to move beyond to the unbelievable sharing in the divine beatitude. And what is that? It might be referred to as sacrifice, which is one way of explaining the meaning of the universe.

Sacrifice is the total giving away of whatever self we have. In the Trinity, God the Father gives himself totally to his Son to such a degree that there is nothing left of him. He becomes nothing while remaining at the same time all potentialities. The Divine Word is like a thought arising in us and becoming crystallized and clear, and then can be expressed like some great inspiration we might have. The Son returns all that he has received from the Father back to the Father in the love of the Holy Spirit. There is nothing in God except the total sacrifice of the divine nature that each divine relationship enjoys. The unity is infinite. The diversity is infinite. And the love is infinite. Love is what unites them. In Heaven, this eternal sacrifice is delightful. Nothing is more delightful than giving oneself totally away.

If we are experiencing God as more intimate and more available, we move to higher levels of consciousness. There is the self we have now, but if we are attached to that, it will be hard to grow beyond it. Like a little box in a bigger box, you have to let yourself be put into a bigger container, so to speak. We are growing in God's Self and in God-consciousness. The ultimate consciousness is the total Oneness in which God is all in all.

So much for the self that becomes God's Self, or one with God's Self, or just plain One. All the mystics agree that that is totally inconceivable. All words can only point in the direction of the Ultimate Reality and the highest experience in this life cannot do justice to "Isness" itself.

The fact of our human weakness will always remain, as Paul describes so eloquently in Romans: "I do what I do not want to do and do not do what I want to do." This is a common experience and has many different manifestations. We cannot ever judge anyone because we do not know what their real motive is. Only God knows what their unconscious motivation is. God is constantly working with us to show us new aspects of our faults and invites us to give them to him. That requires effort on our part, but we gradually become more receptive to the divine psychotherapy. At some point, we do not have to do anything, and the less we do, the more God does.

The idea of effortless contemplative prayer and detachment from all thoughts and even reaching at times the complete silence of awareness without content—this can happen occasionally. The goal is that it happens continuously, not only by consolations in prayer, but in everyday life. As contemplative prayer develops, we are purified of the negative attitudes of trauma that were suppressed for many years, but which still affect our judgments unconsciously, and we cannot do that unless we are reassured that we are not totally bad. In other words, the basic distrust of ourselves, even our good selves, is so deeply immersed in the Christian tradition that it is very hard to get it out.

God has to do something dramatic to shake us out of that mindset. Growing trust in God will be present if we emphasize the positive unconscious with its capacities for union with God and kindness to others.

One aspect of God that is very useful to remember is that he is not one thing. He is not a thing at all. All our ideas with their contradictions and opposites belong to the limitations of rational consciousness. We can make an effort not to be unduly influenced by that background, but it does not fully take away the sense of frustration or even self-hatred that may exist.

The spiritual life, of course, is not about self-hatred. That is a form of pride, not humility. Self-hatred occurs when we do not measure up to the standards in a high-achieving culture like we are in, and which is the education that most people are receiving. It is rather opening to the reality of further evolution that would free theology of some of the negative aspects of the essentialism that emphasizes exclusively God's transcendence. God is infinitely diverse and infinitely One at the same time. The God of creation is totally available and the un-manifest God is totally transcendent. If we do not complete the spiritual life, death will take care of the rest.

We sit together, the mountain and me,
until only the mountain remains.

—L I B A I

CHAPTER FOUR

Christian Non-Duality
and Unity Consciousness

In our discussion of Non-duality, it is important for those committed to the Christian contemplative tradition to think of what Non-duality really means for us. It seems to be a term for enlightenment, transformation, or awakening. It has a very strong conceptual background.

I spoke about sacrifice. The relationships in the Trinity are constantly giving themselves to each other totally so that there is this infinite exchange of love and complete self-sacrifice through the love of the Holy Spirit.

When Christ, the Son of God, by becoming a human entered into humanity, this is the peak of the evolutionary process. The universe becomes conscious of the Creator through human beings who can respond to God with gratitude. Humans become capable of abstract ideas, self-reflection, self-consciousness, forgiving, and compassionate, all of which are not found in the animal kingdom.

In the classical definition of a human being, we are described as "thinking animals." Notice: thinking is only an adjective! So, we are basically mammals, part of this creation, part of this earth, part of this universe, and part of the continuing development of human consciousness.

The idea of Non-duality appears in many of the Christian mystics, in the sacraments, and in the liturgy of the Church. It needs to be more clearly emphasized in our times insofar as this term is the one that is being used in inter-spiritual circles today. In Non-duality the separate-self sense is greatly reduced and even disappears. Everything that happens is the direct experience of reality. It is being able to lead ordinary life without thinking of oneself. When you look at a tree, it is a tree and not you looking at a tree. The latter is the response of our rational intellect.

How do we grow in this new consciousness? Christ became a human being in order to show us how to do this.

Saint Paul compares him to Adam and names him as the Second Adam. The emphasis in Paul's teaching is that all humanity is in Christ in a special way because through his human and divine nature he penetrates with his presence all of humanity, past, present, and to come. Thus, his experience extends to the details of being human, such as eating, having a cup of tea, walking around, taking a bath, sleeping, and whatever ordinary humans have to do to survive and to enjoy life.

Jesus seems to have led an ordinary human life for thirty years. This was his way of manifesting the love of God—becoming one with us in order that human beings might become one with God. One of the classic statements of the Church Fathers was that "God become human in order that the human family might become God."

Jesus reveals this Oneness explicitly in his teaching and especially in his last discourse at the Last Supper where he speaks of oneness with God and with each other. He prays for his followers to be one with the same oneness that he has with the Father and the Father with him. Jesus's Priestly Prayer [John 17] is very strong on our call to oneness with God. Paul develops this insight in his reflections on the Mystical Body of Christ. Through Baptism and grace each human being is invited to become a new creature in Christ as a cell in his Mystical Body. Everything we do in ordinary life cannot be separated from this Oneness. It dwells in us as our deepest self. Little by little, we are meant to develop consciousness of the divine Self by which we were created.

Being aware of ourselves and of God is a kind of duality. Even in the transforming union we are still two. We have to understand what love is.

In the Christian tradition, love is the bottom line: "Love God with your whole heart, mind, soul and strength and your neighbor as yourself." The same God is in others as in us. All humans basically are equal and, if they consent, are inserted into the Mystical Body of Christ to serve each other and to build-up the Body of Christ in every possible way.

Once you are baptized and in grace, you are a living cell in the Body of Christ that has the Holy Spirit as its life blood. The Spirit fills the whole, every cell and, indeed, every particle of every cell.

Teilhard de Chardin said that every particle in the cosmos contains Christ. Since we are made up of trillions of them, we are truly immersed in Christ at all times. In other words, we are saturated with God.

It is not science or intellectual reflection that awakens this reality, of course, but the experience of relating to God in more and more intimate ways so that the ego is no longer dominating. The emotional programs for happiness[1] are laid to rest or moderated so that they are not the main focus of conversation with God or with others.

Duality diminishes like a deep friendship in marriage, where the couple grow more appreciative of each other, bearing with each other's imperfections and limitations. Are these people two or are they more and more one? When Jesus speaks of marriage, he says, that "the two become one flesh." This is certainly a form of Non-duality.

Love is a form of Non-duality that has a personal quality. We belong to the human family and are

1 "Emotional programs for happiness" refers to the idea that all human beings have unmet needs for safety/security, power/control, and affection/esteem. See Thomas Keating, *Invitation to Love* (London: Bloomsbury, 2014).

developing and growing in breadth of perspective and in relationship to God. Christian non-duality then is this increasing merging of all our interests of body, soul, and emotions into the Body of Christ, the New Creation, who through the Spirit has given us the guidance of the Fruits and Gifts of the Spirit. We remain a unique creation, but the limitations of a self at different levels of consciousness disappear into ever greater Oneness but without rejecting the relationships [with God] that we had before. In other words, we are building on previous relationships that were real, but inadequate compared to what transforming union and unity consciousness might be.

The Christian experience of awakening and of unity consciousness is a true Oneness that involves the full participation of our humanity, body, soul, and spirit, distinct from the divine nature, but totally absorbed with the realization of God in the degree that God wills for each of us. A corollary of this is the importance of cultivating an awareness and conviction of the Divine Indwelling. That is really the source and root of the spiritual life: It is here so we do not have to become anybody. We already are all that we can be. When there is nobody to become, how free we will be! We only have to be what we are already, which is the creature and the beloved child of God. Non-duality for the Christian is to be guided by the Spirit, instead of by the false self or the ego.

It is a simple program, but hard to do. All you have to do is nothing. It does not mean that you actually do nothing. It means that you are empty of self-conscious motivation but open to God's action, so that you do what he wants to do. Emptiness is not nothingness, but emptiness with an openness to becoming everything.

I dream of a quiet man who explains nothing . . .
but only knows where the rarest wildflowers are blooming,
and who goes and finds that he is smiling not by his own will.

— WENDELL BERRY

CHAPTER FIVE

The Present Moment and All That Is

O ne advantage that Centering Prayer offers is that it establishes the letting go of self, the total sacrifice of ourselves, as the orientation and direction that grows along with our relationship with God. But, sacrifice in this world is not like it is in Heaven. It can be very difficult, very painful, even unbearable at times. All kinds of difficulties can arise, both socially and emotionally, and spiritually. Faith believes that whatever happens in the present moment is God's will, and the only thing God can will is what is for our greatest good. By letting go of our doubts and turning them over to God, the presence of God begins to grow even in the midst of activity and adversity.

Contemplation and action are not separate, but express themselves according to circumstances. The more broadminded one is, the more firmly established one is in openness to God and to other people. The presence of God relativizes all human experiences in a way that transcends them without necessarily delivering you from the particular aches and pains you are suffering. From the deep strength within us because of the Divine Indwelling, the Spirit gives us the courage, the humility, and the trust to let all happen. The present moment, you might say, is God's way of communicating to us. It's God's texting us, so to speak.

Just as an aside, it might be fun if we briefly review the levels of communication in human history, especially in the last hundred and fifty years. Face-to-face communication is, of course, the most basic one. Then comes writing letters, reading books, the telegram, the telephone, the TV, DVDs, Facebook, Twitter, the cell phone, and texting. We're experiencing a blast of all kinds of communication in a way that no generation ever had to face before. It's a marvelous metaphor of our relationship with God which has no limits and has immense possibilities. The Spirit is suggesting to us what to do in each present moment. We haven't time to think of the past or the future unless God brings them to our attention, because everything that we can genuinely want is NOW. Our capacity is there. God is prepared to fill it, but we just have to go through the experience of development on each level of our progressing humanity, culminating in living just to manifest God in whatever way he calls us to.

In the Body of Christ, as Paul says, there's no good, better, and best. Everything is important. Everything human is God texting us. And the senses, you might say, every one of them, are means in which God is communicating new truths and showing his love for us, inviting us to transcend some or all of our limitations. God's whole being, you might say, is focused on us, as if we were the only creature there was.

So, the present moment, we might say, is the computer through which God is always communicating with us. So, if we think we're alone, we're mistaken. As long as you have your cell phone on, you're in touch with all the world. It's a good symbol of the divine relationship, because in relating to God, you're relating to everything that exists. This is the kind of conviction and conceptual background that we need to insist upon over and over again. We are always in the presence of God and able to stay there and love being there, while submitting to the difficulties and duties or whatever happens at the same time.

Everything is happening in the present moment. It is a Presence that doesn't change, that is always there, and which you contact when contemplative prayer is firmly established. The experience of God can be just a presence, but can also be endlessly varied. Just on the level of the senses, all the physical senses become spiritual senses.

The sense of smell, for example, becomes an attraction towards interior silence and peace; in hearing you melt into a sound; in seeing you melt into the tree; and in touching, God sometimes embraces us or kisses us. Finally, in tasting you experience the inner presence of God, which is both nourishing and delicious. It's that kind of experience that enables the difficulties on the spiritual journey to be overcome, as well as the overwhelming negativity of society, which is going in the opposite direction, faster and faster.

The scientific gadgets mentioned earlier are marvelous metaphors of how many ways God is actually communicating to us at every moment. It's not just a statue or a picture we're thinkingof. It's all of reality contained in its Creator here and now in a single instant. And I'm sure you've noticed questions being raised nowadays: What is time? What is eternity? If it's time at all, it's totally different from our time. And so, time basically is the measure of motion. So, if there's no motion, there's no time. That experience may occur if you're in deep prayer or meditation at times when you're not thinking of anything, but are thoroughly aware of the Presence in whatever form it happens to take in this particular moment. We have to be open to whatever happens as an embrace from God or whatever your favorite sense image may be.

Buddhists recognize a sixth sense which they call the thinking mind. This sense is our chief problem. This faculty needs to be controlled.

Scripture as well as all mystical teachers constantly say to let all thoughts go and let God act. "Let go and let God" is a favorite saying from the AA tradition. We will continue to have thoughts, of course. We need them to function and to plan for the future, but without attachment, without relying on them, and without thinking any old thing. We need to cultivate a certain discipline that enables us to let go of thoughts that are harmful, unkind, or unforgiving and all the other things that are possible in the myriad faculties of a human being.

The awakened state or the non-dual does not think about right and wrong, because such persons are always doing what is the right, because they are under the direct influence of the Spirit. So, there's no need to think of self or the past or to worry about the future but only of now.

That means that Non-duality is really dual consciousness in which you are able to give your whole attention to the duties or expectations, or what the senses are telling us, with all the distractions of life. At the same time, we never leave this conviction—which is not so much an experience as something beyond experience—of a certain certitude that you're always in the presence of God and then you can see God in different things, whatever the Spirit may suggest.

The last thought is this: we stop making efforts to remain in the presence of God and just take everything as it comes. This is to be in the present moment. That's the only place God is. So, if you're there too, then all you have to do is to accept what's happening, or do what God wants you to do about what's happening, believing that you will be guided regardless of how many faults you have. And, in fact, you may rather like your faults, because they keep you humble.

So, what's the point of living? As far as I can see, it's to give God the chance to take over our very complicated human lives and situations completely. Whatever we do is in the service of that project. We don't have to think about it if we are in the present moment. It is happening.

CHAPTER SIX

Fallen, Beloved, Surrendered

A lot of the presentation of the meaning of Jesus's life in the past has been salvation from original sin and its consequences. The meaning of the Fall was that people inherited the sin of Adam and Eve and Jesus was sent by the Father to atone for it. This doctrine is being questioned by theologians today. The full meaning of the Incarnation is being seen in a different perspective.

The present understanding is not just something invented lately. 13th-century Franciscans John Duns Scotus and Saint Bonaventure (among others) had this same idea. Some theologians are leaving behind the whole idea of original sin as not being viable in a contemporary scientific world.

In their opinion, the doctrine is not to be taken historically, but to learn what these events are trying to say. Some are saying that we came out of a level of innocence into a world in which we had to submit to the growth process and the other natural forces that have been scientifically verified.

Following Teilhard de Chardin, the important work that Ilia Delio to make known this vision of creation as a process of evolutionary development that is focused now on the spiritual evolution of human beings. What the doctrine of original sin emphasizes, whatever explanation you give for how it happened, is experienced in all the religions. It is the weakness, vulnerability, self-centeredness, and disregard of the rights and needs of others that characterize the human condition.

It might be liberating to attribute sin largely to our lack of evolution, especially the influence of the emotional programs for happiness developed in early childhood. We would still experience this world as a "fallen" world. Fallen from what? Some theologians propose that we probably were created along with the Word of God emerging from the Father. Everything happens at once in eternity, and maybe everything is happening that ever will happen right now. In any case, the present moment contains all the past and the future.

If human weakness is the result of being un-evolved, it's not responsible even in its so-called free choices. Psychology has shown that veryfew choices are really free and that they are only free to a certain extent due to emotional trauma in childhood and growing up. They only become perfectly free when we die and our brain stops functioning. The brain is habitually and physiologically designed to carry on the habits that we formed in early childhood, circulating around our need to survive and to possess security, to be loved and respected, to be free to experiment with the experience of power and control.

The cross of Christ is a symbol of the human condition, which is rejected by Earth and by Heaven and is sitting in the middle of nowhere as a transitional period from animal consciousnessto angelic or divine consciousness. And so, we couldn't be in a worse place than neither one nor the other, because it means that the animal instincts which we use to survive in this world is a world of senses not controlled by the rational consciousness as it is designed to be, at least according to philosophers like Aristotle, Plato, and Thomas Aquinas. It means that in order to live in this world, you're constantly challenged by tormenting desires: desires of the flesh, desires for intellectual attainments, personality triumphs, and all the things that humans pursue with great urgency, especially wealth, power, and knowledge.

Human nature, in addition, wants to be famous and prominent because such attainments enable us to forget how weak and powerless we actually are.

Belief in creation is the basic foundation of the spiritual journey, along with trust in the Creator God. This has a special term in monastic circles. It was called compunction. It is the experience of our weakness and the overwhelming experience of God's greatness. In other words, it's the acceptance of who we are, which is nobody. We don't have to become anyone, because we already are all that we could possibly be. We possessed it before we became human beings, if you accept the theological idea of the pre-existence of souls in eternity.

At the same time, it's entrusting all our failings to God with confidence in his infinite mercy. It's a balance between our fallen nature and our destiny that has now been given the power through Christ in his Resurrection and the gift of the Spirit to be able to function without dependence on the wrong attitudes of the un-evolved side of our nature.

Sin in Hebrew really means "missing the mark." It's not necessarily a question of guilt. It's simply that you missed the target, which is to be expected. The example is taken from the art of archery. If you miss, fine; try again. You don't expect to succeed, but you keep trying. And it's that trying with many failures that gradually gains a reduction or healing of the obstacles to divine union. In one sense, evolution is just the willingness to learn and keep trying.

Evolution is a concept that involves nature and our human evolution. We have in the brain three levels: the mammalian brain, the human brain, and the spiritual capacity to change. Responses to the frustration of our self-centered desires are programmed into the brain through habitual ways of reacting emotionally.

They are like a mountain that is being eroded. The water heads for the channels that are already in place. The electrical impulses from the senses are interpreted by the brain according to the physiological structure of the synapses and all the other extraordinary capacities of the brain; the bottom line being that we have to get free of those channels, and we need a bulldozer to do the job. Then you can build new channels that are in line with the teaching of the Gospel and practiced virtue. We have to grow into the art of not missing the mark or hitting the bull's-eye. To be on target is to do what the Spirit suggests in each moment without even thinking about it.

You don't forget your identity and you don't avoid using your talents, but there's no attachment to them. One of the great teachings of the Bhagavad Gita is that you are missing the boat if you seek the reward, or even if you seek enlightenment, even if it's God's will for you. If you seek it too vigorously, it's probably an ego trip. That's why all the great mystics say you mustn't be attached to spiritual consolation or ecstasy because the Divine Being is not an object that you love, but a subjective presence that you surrender to. Surrender becomes your main source of motivation, rather than the old self with its infantile, adolescent, and adult preoccupations.

Compunction is the capacity to be more and more humbled by seeing ourselves as we really are: hopelessly defenseless and powerless, but at the same time having an invincible trust that God will take care of it. Even surrender is God's gift. It's more exact to say surrendered. This is the disposition of Christ in his agony in the Garden of Gethsemane. He didn't want to go through it. But he said, "Not my will, but Thine be done." There are trials so intense that they can break down one's usual peace of mind.

God is calling us to a new level of consciousness that requires going through a new depth of detachment. Self-knowledge is the classical term for this process in the Christian mystical tradition. Humility is recognizing who we actually are—powerless—and not be distressed by it and even to feel contentment with it. Confidence in God will then grow faster and deeper.

We do not obtain gifts by going in search of them,

but by waiting for them to appear.

—SIMONE WEIL

FURTHER REFLECTIONS
by Thomas Keating

If you want to pray...

Centering Prayer responds to this invitation:

> by consenting to God's presence and action within
> by surrendering our will completely to God
> by relating to God who dwells in secret, which is
> the silence of self.

As God brings the "new creation" to life in interior silence, that is to say, the new you, with the worldview that Christ shares in deep silence, his view of things becomes more important than our own. Then God asks us to live that new life in the circumstances of everyday life, contradicted by turmoil, opposition and anxieties of all kinds.

–Open Mind, Open Heart

Contemplative prayer is a process of interior transformation, a conversion initiated by God and leading, if we consent, to divine union. One's way of seeing reality changes in this process.

A restructuring of consciousness takes place which empowers one to perceive, relate, and respond to everyday life with increasing sensitivity to the divine presence in, through, and beyond everything that happens.

–*Open Mind, Open Heart*

A creative vision releases an enormous amount of
energy and can transform society beyond our wildest
dreams. Divine empowerment is present.
…The power of the stars is nothing compared to the
energy of a person whose will has been freed from the
false-self system and who is thus enabled to co-create
the cosmos together with God. …Maybe it will be
a little different tomorrow.

–Open Mind, Open Heart

"Jesus shows us what it means to be a human person and the way to deepen our humanity toward the fullness of life. His disciples recognized him as the Christ, the anointed One...the One who will bring about a new future, a new creation, and who has already done so in our present age...What took place in Jesus' life must take place in ours as well if the fullness of Christ is to come to be."

—ILIA DELIO, *THE EMERGENT CHRIST*

Guidelines for Christian Life, Growth, and Transformation

from Open Mind, Open Heart

THE FOLLOWING PRINCIPLES REPRESENT a tentative effort to restate the Christian spiritual journey in contemporary terms. They are designed to provide a conceptual background for the practice of Centering Prayer. They should be read one at a time, slowly and reflectively as a spiritual practice, according to the method of *Lectio Divina*.[1]

The fundamental goodness of human nature, like the mystery of the Trinity, Grace, and the Incarnation, is an essential element of Christian faith. This basic core of goodness is capable of unlimited development; indeed, of becoming transformed into Christ and deified.

---

1 *Lectio Divina* is a contemplative practice that involves "reading, reflecting, responding, and resting in" a short passage of text. See Julie Saad, *Contemplative Life: Discovering Our Path into the Heart of God* (Balboa Press, 2021), pp 81-106.

Our basic core of goodness is our True Self. Its center of gravity is God. The acceptance of our basic goodness is a quantum leap in the spiritual journey.

✳

God and our True Self are not separate. Though we are not God, God and our True Self are the same thing.

✳

The term original sin is a way of describing the human condition, which is the universal experience of coming to full reflective self-consciousness without the certitude of union with God. This gives rise to our intimate sense of incompletion, dividedness, isolation, and guilt.

✳

Original sin is not the result of personal wrongdoing on our part. Still, it causes a pervasive feeling of alienation from God, from other people and from the True Self. The cultural consequences of these alienations are instilled in us from earliest childhood and passed on from one generation to the next. The urgent need to escape from the profound insecurity of this situation gives rise, when unchecked, to insatiable desires for pleasure, possession, and power. On the social level, it gives rise to violence, war, and institutional injustice.

✳

This constellation of pre-rational reactions is the foundation of the false self. The false self develops in opposition to the True Self. Its center of gravity is itself.

✳

Grace is the presence and action of Christ at every moment of our lives. The sacraments are ritual actions in which Christ is present in a special manner, confirming and sustaining the major commitments of our Christian life.

✳

Personal sin is the refusal to respond to Christ's self-communication (grace). It is the deliberate neglect of our own genuine needs and those of others. It reinforces the false self.

✳

In Baptism, the false self is ritually put to death, the new self is born and the victory over sin won by Jesus through his death and Resurrection is placed at our disposal. Not our uniqueness as persons, but our sense of separation from God and from others is destroyed in the death-dealing and life-giving waters of Baptism.

✳

The Eucharist is the celebration of life: the coming together of all the material elements of the cosmos, their emergence to consciousness in human persons, and the transformation of human consciousness into divine consciousness. It is the manifestation of the Divine in and through the Christian community. We receive the Eucharist in order to become the Eucharist.

※

Our basic core of goodness is dynamic and tends to grow of itself. This growth is hindered by the illusions and emotional hang-ups of the false self, by the negative influences coming from our cultural conditioning, and by personal sin.

※

Listening to God's word in Scripture and the liturgy, waiting upon God in prayer, and responsiveness to his inspirations help to distinguish how the two selves are operating in particular circumstances.

※

God is not some remote, inaccessible, and implacable Being who demands instant perfection from his creatures and of whose love we must make ourselves worthy. He is not a tyrant to be obeyed out of terror, nor a policeman who is ever on the watch, nor a harsh judge ever ready to apply the verdict of guilty. We should relate to him less and less in terms of reward and punishment and more and more on the basis of the gratuity—or the play—of divine love.

✳

The experience of being loved by God enables us to accept our false self as it is, and then to let go of it and journey to our True Self. The inward journey to our True Self is the way to divine love.

✳

The growing awareness of our True Self, along with the deep sense of spiritual peace and joy which flow from this experience, balances the psychic pain of the disintegrating and dying of the false self. As the motivating power of the false self diminishes, our True Self builds the new self with the motivating force of the divine love.

✳

The building of our new self is bound to be marked by innumerable mistakes and sometimes by sin. Such failures, however serious, are insignificant compared to the inviolable goodness of our True Self. We should ask God's pardon, seek forgiveness from those we may have offended, and then act with renewed confidence and energy as if nothing had happened.

※

Prolonged, pervasive, or paralyzing guilt feelings come from the false self. True guilt in response to personal sin or social injustice does not lead to discouragement but to amendment of life. It is a call to conversion.

※

Progress in the spiritual journey is manifested by the unconditional acceptance of other people, beginning with those with whom we live.

※

A community of faith offers the support of example, correction and mutual concern in the spiritual journey. Above all, participating in the mystery of Christ through the celebration of the liturgy, praying the scriptures, and silent prayer binds the community in a common search for transformation and union with God. The presence of Christ is ministered to each other and becomes tangible in the community, especially when it is gathered for worship or engaged in some work of service to those in need.

❋

The moderation of the instinctual drives of the developing human organism for survival and security, affection and esteem, control and power allows true human needs to come into proper focus. Primary among these needs is intimacy with another or several human persons. By intimacy is meant the mutual self-disclosure of thoughts, feelings, problems and spiritual aspirations, which gradually develops into spiritual friendship.

❋

Spiritual friendship involving genuine self-disclosure is an essential ingredient for happiness both in marriage and in the celibate lifestyle. The experience of intimacy with another or several persons expands and deepens our capacity to relate to God and to everyone else. Under the influence of divine love the sexual energy is gradually transformed into universal compassion.

*

The spiritual radiation of a community depends on the commitment of its members to the transformational journey and to each other. To offer one another space in which to grow as persons is an integral part of this commitment.

*

Contemplative prayer, in the traditional sense of the term, is the dynamic that initiates, accompanies and brings the process of transformation to completion.

*

Reflection on the Word of God in Scripture and in our personal history is the foundation of Centering Prayer The spontaneous letting go of particular thoughts and feelings in prayer is a sign of progress. Centering Prayer is characterized not so much by the absence of thoughts and feelings as by detachment from them.

*

The goal of genuine spiritual practice is not the rejection of the good things of the body, mind, or spirit, but the right use of them. No aspect of human nature or period of human life is to be rejected, but integrated into each successive level of unfolding self-consciousness. In this way, the partial goodness proper to each stage of human development is preserved and only its limitations are left behind. The way to become divine is thus to become fully human.

※

The practice of a spiritual discipline is essential at the beginning of the spiritual journey as a means of developing the foundations of the contemplative dimension of life: dedication and devotion to God and service to others.

※

Regular periods of silence and solitude quiet the psyche, foster interior silence and initiate the dynamic of self-knowledge.

※

Solitude is not primarily a place, but an attitude of total commitment to God. When one belongs completely to God, the sharing of one's life and gifts continually increases.

※

The beatitude of poverty of spirit springs from the increasing awareness of our True Self. It is a non-possessive attitude toward everything and a sense of unity with everything at the same time. The interior freedom to have much or to have little and the simplifying of one's lifestyle are signs of the presence of poverty of spirit.

※

Chastity enhances and expands the power to love. It perceives the sacredness of everything that is. As a consequence, one respects the dignity of other persons and cannot use them merely for one's own fulfillment.

※

Obedience is the unconditional acceptance of God as he is and as he manifests himself in our lives. God's will is not immediately evident. Docility inclines us to attend to all the indications of his will. Discernment sifts the evidence and then decides, in the light of the inward attraction of grace, what God seems to be asking here and now.

※

Humility is an attitude of honesty with God, oneself, and all reality. It enables us to be at peace in the presence of our powerlessness and to rest in the forgetfulness of self.

✳

Hope springs from the continuing experience of God's compassion and help. Patience is hope in action. It waits for the saving help of God without giving up, giving in, or going away.

✳

The disintegrating and dying of our false self is our participation in the passion and death of Jesus. The building of our new self, based on the transforming power of divine love, is our participation in his risen life.

✳

In the beginning, emotional hang-ups are the chief obstacle to the growth of our new self because they put our freedom into a straight jacket. Later, because of the subtle satisfaction that springs from self-control, spiritual pride becomes the chief obstacle. And finally, reflection of self becomes the chief obstacle because this hinders the innocence of divine union.

✳

Human effort depends on grace even as it invites it. Whatever degree of divine union we may reach bears no proportion to our effort. It is the sheer gift of divine love.

✳

Jesus did not teach a specific method of meditation or bodily discipline for quieting the imagination, memory, and emotions. We should choose a spiritual practice adapted to our particular and natural disposition. We must also be willing to dispense with it when called by the Spirit to surrender to his direct guidance. The Spirit is above every method or practice. To follow his inspiration is the sure path to perfect freedom.

✳

What Jesus proposed to his disciples as the Way is his own example: the forgiveness of everything and everyone and the service of others in their needs. His final teaching:"Love one another as I have loved you."

ABOUT THE AUTHOR

Beloved Trappist monk Thomas Keating is best known as one of the primary founders of the Centering Prayer movement, which made the contemplative dimension of Christianity accessible through a simple method of silent, still meditation. He is also known as the convener of the Snowmass Interreligious Conference, which helped spawn the global Inter-spiritual movement. Keating's open invitation to people of all walks to embark on a spiritual journey, coupled with his emphasis on the oneness of all creation, made him a 20th century harbinger of 21st century ideals.

SUPPORTING INDIGENOUS FUTURES
1% GIVEN BACK

Wayfarer Books is based in the San Juan Mountains near Mesa Verde, on the lands of the Ancestral Pueblo, the Southern Ute, the Weenuche (Mountain Ute), the Diné (Navajo), and the San Juan Southern Paiute Tribe. We honor the generations of Indigenous communities who have stewarded these lands for thousands of years. We acknowledge that this place was taken through genocide, colonization, and displacement. We respect the Indigenous peoples who remain here, both past and present. As one concrete act of accountability, we are launching 1% Given Back. Beginning in 2026, we will give 1% of Wayfarer's net profits directly to the Indigenous nations on whose lands we are based, in support of sovereignty, Indigenous futures, and wealth redistribution. We do this in the belief that acknowledgment should move beyond words and into tangible practice.

LEARN MORE AT WAYFARERBOOKS.ORG

At Wayfarer Books we believe poetry is the language of the earth. We believe words, like rivers through wild places, can change the shape of the world. We publish poets and writers and renegades who stand outside of mainstream culture; poets, essayists, and storytellers whose work might withstand the scrutiny of crows and coyotes, those who are cryptic and floral, the crepuscular, and the queer-at-heart. We are more than just a publisher but a community of writers. Our mission is to produce books that can serve as a compass and map to all wayfarers through wild terrain.

WAYFARERBOOKS.ORG